Cantos from a Cage.
Poems of Lockdown.

Jeff Rich

ISBN: 978-0-6451592-6-4 (Print)

ISBN: 978-0-6451592-7-1 (E-Book)

jeffrich.substack.com

Melbourne, Australia

Table of Contents

Author's Introduction

In the years of the coronavirus pandemic from 2020 to 2022, the world conducted a great experiment, and the imaginative soul was secluded in a great trial. In these years of health and order, large portions of the world experienced deprivations of normal human freedoms. We were locked down, shut down, and mandated. We were masked, vaccinated, tested and controlled. We were instructed daily from political leaders and journalists from a newly omnipotent bully pulpit. We were treated by public health physicians who never dared to ask us how we were feeling. We were all put in a cage.

I will not belabour the details since we all had our own intense experience of this great collective trauma and ecstatic communion. Memory, history and forgetting will do its work over time to forge coherent narratives of this global event. But we all also know that this experience was more chaotic dream than coherent narrative. Through the dream, voices from spectres we could not touch called out to us in our lonely night. Many people celebrated the sanity of this cage. Some called out to their fellow prisoners in hate. Others rattled the cage in anger. Some were defeated by sadness in the cage. Some, even many, suffered bitter, lonely, sanitised deaths in this cage.

In my cage, I turned to poetry, in flight from my daily trade as a minor official in the bureaucracy that had locked up the world. I have written in prose elsewhere, in *Thirteen Ways of Looking at a Bureaucrat: Writings on Government* of my journal of these plague years. There I wrote about my own attempts to make sense of the Great Seclusion, the social changes wrought by the pandemic, and the totalitarian virus that had infected the world. I wrote as an outsider locked up in an insider's cage. Though a minor official in a health department that pursued some of the world's most zealous Zero COVID policies, I criticised those policies. I disagreed openly and directly. I felt the shadow of power fall over my life as a result. I found myself not in one cage, but in three. I was locked down in the cage of public health rules, banished in the cage for blacklisted bureaucrats, and confined in a cage for dreamers of forbidden, mad thoughts. In these three cages, the whispered voices of my madness and incoherent poetry were my refuge and escape. With them I breathed through all three layers of iron bars and joined the infinite conversation of humanity's incantations and fables.

In this time, I turned in my weak songs to inspiration to a tainted master and tortured monster, Ezra Pound, and his *Pisan Cantos*. If, as I believe, modernism was a Renaissance of the twentieth century, then Ezra Pound is one of the greatest but most troubling figures of that cultural renewal. His poetry reached across cultures and centuries like a prophet in a tower. He was the great progenitor, and the great impresario of early modernist poetry. It was Pound that Eliot honoured as the greater maker in *The Wasteland*. But Pound's poetry was stained by both his politics and his madness. He became infected by earlier strains of totalitarian, hateful and deluded thought. Overshadowing his poetic achievements, including the magnificent difficult music of the *Cantos*, were his failures as a man of judgement. He broadcast for Mussolini. He filled the Cantos with rants on his political theories and tributes to obscure economic principles of social credit theory. The Americans captured him at the end of the war. They sought his conviction as a traitor. He was kept in a prisoner of war camp. There, caged outside Pisa, in the arid ruins of Europe, he sang the broken magnificent threnody of *Canto LXXXI*: what thou lovest well shall not be reft from thee.

Pound was ultimately spared the death sentence by a sentence of insanity. Legal specialists in psychiatry and criminal psychopathy still discuss his trial and his case. There remains controversy about his stay in St Elizabeth's lunatic asylum. Was he mad? Was he bad? Was his poetry the mind of poison or of greatness? Was the salon he kept an indulgence? Were the poets who gathered around him, and forgave him his misjudgements, naive fools, willing traitors, unwitting collaborators with the atrocities of antisemitism?

But this pariah poet inspired me in the time of lockdowns and seclusion Why? Neither acclaim nor ostracism can extinguish the voice. Neither tradition nor its breaking can constrain the voice. Neither madness nor politics can define the voice. Out of the cages of our lives, we sing our greatest cantos.

I survived the years of the pandemic by claiming my voice as an author. I sang the dark cantos from a cage that I have assembled in this collection. These were poems that met deeper, more urgent needs than publication. They were performances of their time, and to burnish them into perfection now would be to betray them. I present them to you as the imperfect words of the spirits who passed through me in those years. I do not know any more if the same self that wrote these poems inhabits this body of mine. I dare not judge or condemn or spend too much time editing these poems. They are somewhere between poetry and a diary of the torment we all experienced during the pandemic. I share them as a contribution to the understanding of that experience, not as admission to the union of professional poets.

The poems are arranged in four parts.

In *Sleep Machine*, I gather poems from the early period of the pandemic. In early 2020, I began to use a CPAP (continuous positive airway pressure) machine to treat my long-standing problems with sleep apnoea and snoring. These poems evoke the image of a machine breathing new life into this ageing writer, and teaching this tattered cloak upon a stick, to sleep, and then to clap his soul into action. It became a metaphor for our society as a whole.

In *Cantos from a Cage,* I record my mental experience of enduring the long lockdowns in Melbourne. Between 2020 and 2022 this city in Southeastern Australia suffered the world's longest lockdown. These poems echo parts of Pound's own *Cantos*, though not at all systematically. They were written not for eternity, but to survive this long internment.

In *Other Songs,* I gather several other poems written between 2020 and 2023, including some poems written in response to the open war between Russia and the West in Ukraine.

In *Garden Tanka,* I have collected most of the *tanka* I wrote as a form of healing during the long confinements in our private houses and gardens. The *tanka* is a form of Japanese poetry, from which the shorter haiku form was adapted. *Tanka* consist of five lines, in English language versions, written in a syllabic count of

5-7-5-7-7. Through these *tankas* I slowly left my cage.

I closed the collection with these garden *tankas* because they point to the green shoots emerging from the ruin of our culture after the pandemic. Like Voltaire, I have long believed that when the world falls apart, as it always does, it is best to tend one's garden. As I assemble this collection, I know my garden is thriving, but I do not know if I will ever publish another collection of poetry. Vaclav Havel once observed that it is theoretically possible that within the week he might write his best play ever. And that it was also possible that he might never write again. If I never write poetry again, I am forever in debt to these songs, which I have transcribed here, because they saved my soul when our democracies died again in darkness.

In mid-2025 I added a revised Afterword to explain my long delay in publishing these poems.

The Poems

The Sleep Machine

The Sleep Machine

This human can't even sleep,
not without a machine to help,

by pumping fresh breath into my neck,
To keep the air pipe from succumbing.

Not without a mask over my face,
umbilical cord to the CPAP,

like some old god slave from a game
who searches for madness in abandoned
dreams.

I submit to the prescribed pressure;
float through the blessed portals

into the infinite conversation;
the braids of the old traditions

that augment this dreaming brain
to reach across the dark boundary.

The Mask

I connect through the transparent mask.
Trigger autostart with the first breath.

The first gasp creates a suction cup,
a short panic of asphyxiation,

while expelled air learns to escape
this prison I evaded for decades.

I enter the augmented world
where dream rejoins machine

to return the night to silence,
to make morning the green dawn.

When I stretch out to my mind,
I see a city rising in the plain;

I begin the march to its outer gates,
And I speak once more in bells.

Quarantine

There is nowhere to go.
Stay at home
For forty days, maybe more.

Quarantena. Lockdown.
Shut it all down,
they say, who do not roam

in this desert without bounds.
Lost. Parched. But no fever.
We march alone relentlessly.

We wait for the daily orders
of mad epidemiologists
who turn models of illness

into rules for life.
What if they are wrong?
Of course, they are wrong.

Aren't we all?
We have lost our illusions:
we had imagined our world

free of error,

spared from infection,
elevated above borders.

But nature's demon made a zoonotic leap
into our brittle cities.
Screamed: I am the master now.

The virus is a language.
We stammer out its meanings
in our solitary cells.

We try to master the miasma,
cloak our orifices,
cleanse our vulnerable touch.

Keep our distance,
Even from the ones we love.
All on faith that some doctor

said this will work.
Whatever the cost,
do it! Ward off death.

On Zoom, we cannot smell the fear.
We pretend to carry on
as if the war will be over by Christmas.

And none know when it will end.
Only that medical science
Will soon find a cure, if not a vaccine.

Until then, we obey;
count each tolling bell;
learn that death diminishes me.

Lockdown

If you can tell lies, you must stay home.
If you can live your life, you must stop now.
If you want to free your heart, you must lock
down.
And if you lock down, the mad doctors will
not let you out.

If you can model numbers, you must derange
hope.
If you can wash your hands, you must follow
the rules.
If you can read a chart, you must make
forecasts,
then deny they were predictions
when they all go wrong.

If you can cede control, you must give up.
Follow the doctors orders.
Make your way slowly through the queue.
Comply. Distance. Hide.
Shelter in their mistake.

The social police will hunt you down.
Test you.

Trace each and every contact
your dark blue tooth recognises.
Then, count your case to justify

an epidemiologist's dream:
that statistics can save the world.
That care matters less than rules.
That the public health crowd know the future.

One month they called us fools
because we panicked when the shelves were
bare.
Do they countenance their own folly?
How the whole world screamed at a mouse?

When our leaders fitted people to a sigmoid
curve
to flatten the uncertainty of death?
Why they relived the Spanish flu of textbooks,
first as tragedy, and then as farce?

The Way Out Machine

In the distance, we keep for fear,
I enclose my breath in a mask
to pump hope into my lungs.

I begin to dream
of the way out machine
that will free us from

The dictatorship of the physicians.

Curfew, Melbourne 2020

Unimaginable city, locked down in its dark
tomb,
its streets masked for an uncommon cold.

Now all movement, all strangeness stops at 8
pm.
Some turn in, from fear; we turn inward, in
defiance.

We will not be interred within five kilometres
of home.
Not by the impatient doctors and erring
statisticians,

who mutter the words
of some defunct military strategist:

*"This will be a campaign unlike any other in
history.
"A campaign characterized by shock,
by surprise, by ... overwhelming force."*

A population cowers in unhealthy awe
at the daily tacking of Captain Ahab.

Eliminate the white whale, he cries.
Hunt it down, with the genomic trace.

But the crew never could comprehend
the captain's crazed commands.

The epi harpoon never could slay
the majesty of nature.

So, when the whale's tail clapped
the ocean into a wave,

the *Pequod* was split;
we sank to this dark ocean floor.

RNA-seething city, city full of dead dreams,
where ghosts by daylight tug passing sleeves

to ask: can the captain raise
this dismasted wreck?

Are we doomed to prowl
the cold dim ocean floor

Until the miracle appears,

and death, decay and illness
Disappear from this world?
Just like joy did?

Just like we lost all chance encounters?
When for forty nights, the gifts of strangers

were banned from this distanced city,
whose undead citizens shelter in silenced
vengeance.

An Aubade

Silent 5 am starts disarm fatigue.
Once I could not bestir myself
in this morning darkness.

Now the hissing mask
releases the pressure of dreams
into the inexplicable day.

Light flows in.
Illness eases its way past,
while my own lungs repair,

and begin unaided to breathe.
The night lets go of me;
and I let go, in the day.

The Melbourne Captivity

The Lord said:
How long will ye sin?
How long will thy nature defy the orders?
How long will ye let sickness inhabit the
earth?

The people said:
We are locked down in our shame
And confusion covers our face
For we have sinned against the Law.

The Lord said:
I have driven them into their homes
In mine anger, and in my great wrath.
I will cause them to dwell safely.

The people said:
We will endure this captivity.
Yet we will not relinquish all freedom
Since, in the nights of curfew, we dream of touch.

The Lord said
I will put my fear into their hearts.
Can you even find one honest man

Who walks among the people without his
mask?

Ezra stood among the people and said:
What thou lovest well will not be reft from thee.
Now is the time to repeat great words;
Walk away from the golden chains.

The Lord remained silent when questioned.
His Babylon soon fell.

Breathless

Could it be the new coronavirus?
Or merely the old common cold?

Should I get tested, or resist
the reckless screams of data collectors?

After all, chances are it is just hayfever,
and my body is not about to collapse

in the terror of the cytokine storm.
Even the reigning doctors cannot name

the symptoms that ail me most.
This interminable house arrest.

Exile from the dying city.
White gowns, black masks.

Smothered and breathless.
Shackled by a five k chain.

Condemned to meet only avatars
while the last post plays.

In the forbidden distance,
priests prepare the rites.

They chant:
"Not this, not this."

The Personal is Poetical

The personal is poetical,
and not a domain to be ruled.

It shatters on contact with power.
Slides away from shouts on streets.

Seeks out soft silent shelters
where, in a parliament of shadows,

strange freedom speaks its mind.
Then, in an unplanned shaft of light,

the shattered self reassembles.
It rises in a spiral of words:

not on the stone columns of Cicero;
not by Antifa's fists and fires;

but lifted in light circles out of hell,
on the wings of a terrible angel.

La Noche Oscura

Not darkness, obscurity.
Not shadow, life with no light.

Not grasping at goals, but falling into the
chasm.
Not knowing the secrets, but shattering the
lies from which we drink truth.

Not blinded in black, but hidden in light.
Not loss alone, but loss that liberates.

Not denial of the real, but refusal to attach.
Not staggering down the untraveled road,

lost in the circles,
without knowing where to walk.

Not sure in safety, but imperilled in obscurity.
Not known in this fragile world,

but searching
for more urgent longings.

Not insanity, madness.

Not despair. Revelation in doubt.

Not the path to death, but infinite birth.
Not my last night, but kindness at dawn.

Silence

Locked down in silence for too long,
waiting for the pandemic to pass

into its endemic certainty,
when shock and awe will be known

as the health war crime of this year,
when the victims - and we are all victims -

turn on the generals of elimination,
the curfew physicians,

the quisling bureaucrats
(liars, cowards, executioners all),

tear the black masks from their face,
throw them into a cornered cell,

demand they sign the confession,
and put a vaccine to their heads.

Two Voices Vie in My Head

Two voices vie in my head:

You must fight and take arms
against the inquisitors of the plague.

You must withdraw behind unsappable walls
to rewrite the City of God without faith

Two generals order my march:

Hold this trench we dug for you
when you were a private with no arms.

Be like Kutuzov; burn this Moscow,
so the soul released at Borodino may live.

Two claims contest my heart:

Stand with Max's ethic of responsibility.
Win over the courtiers who despise me.

Accept my defeat to win the peace of truth,
and there stand in the sun, dangerous.

No One is Listening

No-one is listening, not when I write
No-one is listening, not even now
No-one is listening, when the titans close in
on speech
No-one is listening, as the culture bleeds out
No-one is listening, but all stake out their
mikes
No-one is listening, when the dying trees sing
their threnodies
No-one is listening, when the last book is born
No-one is listening, while asphyxiation rises
through the steam

House Arrest

They locked down our minds
Before they locked down our homes
They stripped purpose from life,
Then put a mask on our face.

Eucalyptus

I walk the linear track
along the restored creek.
Reach out to crush
the arc leaf beneath my nose

Shimmering drapes over twisted
white wax spines
who contort in the heat,
stained by their bleeding sap.

These familiars misguide my way
when *mimesis* fills my ear;
when the origin tale of the West
holds its knife at my own throat.

And I wonder: what forms
do these dying generations
whisper beneath the wind?
Woken by an angel in flight?

Metered Sleep

My metered sleep is imperfect.
The blue light instructs me each day
on the frequency of my nightly faults.

A good night is under five.
A great night is under two.
But in last night the machine

was no salve. Arousal drove
Me mad. My lungs suckered
the rubber in a sweat.

Only the promise of the sun,
saluted with a folding bow,
returned me to rest,

consecrated the body in the mind.

To the Sea

Can I board the ship this late?
The winds lull and my shoulders sag.
This morning no words come to the captain.

Only, this long regret:
for all the years enslaved to fear.
Still my mind, and say farewell

to the harbour 's painted stores.
You never were my home, I say.
You will not be my longer grave.

Pack only a seven kilo bag.
Bless my bitter enemies.
They dismissed me too long ago.

Cross the gangplank
to float like a dancer across
the churning sea.

Never hold this chain again.
Leave it at the fleeing pier,
where rust will do, what will cannot.

Cantos from a Cage

Canto I

In a locked down city
Enduring three seasons of hell
I turn to you, *il miglio fabbro*
To guide me from this cage.

The Pisan camp
Is a waste of space
I am lost in this cage.

Only my devices for company.
The oligarchs spy on my thoughts.
The whirlwind blows to Charter '77.

From a prison
Vaclav wrote
Letters to Olga.

I've discovered that in lengthy prison terms
sensitive people are in danger
of becoming embittered
developing grudges against the world
growing dull, indifferent and selfish.
One of my main aims
is not to yield an inch to such threats

regardless of how long I'm here.
I want to remain open to the world
not to shut myself up against it
I want to retain my interest in other people
and my love for them.

Awaiting executioners
Boethius found consolation
In the infinite conversation.

No affliction can sever me from my God
And the angels of his verse…

But the flawed Prophet Ezra
Spoke of the children of Israel
Come again out of captivity.

Fasted. Distanced,
From the filth
Of this land's heathen.

Made isolate
Out of madness
He shouted silent dissent
Through his barred cage
Under his mask.

They told me I was everything:
'tis a lie, I am no ague-proof.

Show me, great maker,
How to pound these words into meal.
Prepare me for the sacrifice.

The trial to come
Will arraign my identity.
Just as they asked of you:

Traitor? Madman? Mere poet?
Dilettante in ideas
You had no say in?

To think the republic could allow
You to speak and recite
The words of the elder Adams.

'Americans are more rapidly
Disposed to corruption in elections.'

I am abandoned
On the River Styx.
The Upper World denies me burial rites.

Where is my Agamemnon?
Who will defy the tyrant
When his singers inspire fear?

The last boat left for quarantine.
We are banned
From leaving this land.

Under the shadow
Of the great virus,
I must come to love my prison.

The twisted snow gum.
The treasure of books.
The birds of Messiaen's song.

They do not need
My cold breath.
Not even they can console me.

I saw Persephone
Walk by
In a glass carriage.

Only a few seeds

Of the pomegranate
Now, but power,

In this realm of death,
Claims her,
Pulls her Down,

Checks her in,
Chains her here
Before mine blind mouth.

The Styx becomes the Brisbane
In my song.
I watch the muddy waters

Rise.
Claim all that
I could call home.

Show me, prophet.
Show me, maker.
Show me the way from this cage.

The sacred mountain waits,
Enters the sky.
Throw your stone on the mound.

Drink down all your shame.
Leave the stupor that numbs all of us.
Burn your mask.

No longer speak in whispers
Of the Yezhovian terror in Leningrad,
Of lines languishing in the fountain.

'How long must I wait
For the execution?'

The virus clasps the fetters of the Self.
Sing a song of distance
A RAT-kit full of lies.

278 days in medical arrest.
'Can you describe this?'
120 Days of Sodom.

I watch my jailer
Speak from Treasury Place
In the screens of my cage.

Lead me from this place, Ezra.
With your madness dissolve the key.
Take me on a night journey from this cage.

Canto II

And yet beauty remains
It endures through
All the chants of change.

And demands to be spoken
Even from within this prison
From this cage concealed in my garden.

The dichter, the skald, the magus
Insist from Boethius' cell,
Against wracked screams,
That philosophy consoles,
Lights our way still.

Speaking insists.
It will not be isolated.
Call that going. Call that on.

Interior freedom.
The cardinal spent nine years in solitary.
He converted the guards.

Solzhenitsyn survived the gulag.
And knew evil

Ran through his own heart.

The chains the jailer reset on our ankles
Do not constrain our minds.
There is no power in this cage.

Canto III

The dark angels visited Lygon Street
The *ristorantes* of youth are all closed.
Donnini's, Trotters, Cantuccio.

The University Hotel is gutted
Repurposed as betting shop,
convenience store up for lease.

My lost connections
linger here on the street.

I peer at the dark, messy inside
Abandoned after my youth
Broken on the wheel of public health.

And the Dane said
This simple truth:
To live is to feel oneself lost.

Like the shipwreck of John Clare's mind
The toll of mobility in the Victorian age
We search for something to cling to.

To bring order

To the chaos.
To order the rage of the sea.

'These are the only genuine ideas,
The ideas of the shipwrecked.'

Canto IV

And the Dread Angel spoke at night:
You will never hear of my time
My place, my people, my flight.

Our stories, our shame, our glory.
All is now oblivion.
The memory-killers have won.

And the Dread Angel sang:
I am not bound by place.
I have been elevated above the earth.

I uproot my soul and
scatter like a wind
across so many lands,

I do not care
about belonging.
Can we belong

To the conquered blood
that waters the earth
of every homeland?

Can we belong
to the fires that dispossess
these groves of deception?

And Isaac the Syrian said

How small psychic life is
When compared with the hope
Preserved for eternities.

The Great German said

Be as wise as the wise ones of this world
Yet at any moment know you may find yourself
Walking like a child into the darkness.

Canto V

No-one sings for the official.
He slides to the back of shot.
The captive official,
singer in his gilded cage,
slinks from the camera,
hides from the unimportant,
and the untitled.
He keeps his fame close
for high status gamers only.

I am scholar and outcast,
Confucius searching
to find the good Zhou,
who might restore
ritual in a desacralised world.
Exile in borderlands.
Scholarship itself outcast.

They locked the iron gate again,
in a panic to save their skins.
Now the slightest puff of wind
carries this virus beyond their lies.

This generation dies young too.

They yearn for sunshine
and water to fill its tap root
that stretches to find
the buried nutrients of the past.

Canto VI

I garden in the ruins.
Relieve captivity with a garden view.
Some fragments of Japanese design,

the three stones
arranged as islands
on this clay-baked sea.

Kangaroo paw flares.
The wattle bleeds early
this not Spring

stained
by our own
imagining.

In spring the birds swoop and give chorus
To all the forgotten wells of love
And the mowers return.

The buzz cutters of the local council
Fill the curfewed street with maintenance.
These locked down streets begin

To breathe, without masks again.
The imprisonment by press conference is
over.
Now, all the neglected gardens

Are set to order
once more by machines.
Yet in the harsh blue Sunday

I can only hear, in quavers and stanzas,
The whistles of lorikeets,
The loving coo-coos of a native dove.

The shaded corner where shrubs
do never grow
Is where I sometimes sit on the ochre dais,

empty and powerless.
I dream there of Ezra's prophecy,
His ambition in the Cantos

To hold a dying culture
together with the songs
of its enchantment

Canto VII

The American preachers and oligarchs
are at War again, for another year.
They want to declare the China Sea
their Manifest Destiny Pond.

Red Eyes and sounds of war
remember the sleepless dream.
War is coming, Cassandra cries.
Exiled on this island home,
We smother ourselves in public health.

Golden Wattle clouds float near red tears.
I am falling into the damp prison.
Walls crumble.
Devastation cultures.

They can make us back down.
They can take our lives.
They can even take our freedom.
At least, they proved that.
Sorry, Melbourne.

Australia has fallen.
Australia has fallen.

I chanted

Then, I knew
I was mad.

Dr Cogito went back
to delete his tweets

Canto VIII

Do not watch the sunset.

My life became a *Downfall* parody.

In the years of the Andrews Terror
I could not even gather
outside the Leningrad Prison.

I walked down the street
without my obedience mask.
I gave in to the human instinct
to act friendly to passers by.

I was consigned to nothing.
Tasked to futility.
Like Ezra I made broadcasts
To stave in my madness.

Venom towards the journalists.
Sarcasm at the supine.

Longing to be heard,
to get a hashtag running

The smart-suited reporter in his bubble
Of to-camera vision

Is Spotted by the protesting crowd.
And in revenge or in response

Or just in freedom
They stand at the free space

The cameraman sought to exploit
To show the crowd diminished

As background to the shot.
But the crowd shouts the suiter singer

Of the regime down,
'Tell the Truth.'

'Run away.' 'We want the truth.'
'Go home. Go home.'

Cheers and boos break out
When the police persuade
The cub in his over-smart suit
To walk away. To let it go.
He will have to rely on empty lies,

Deprived of his framing shot.

In the Spring the crowds began
To swarm the CBD.
Or so said, the regime puppets
Who played on their strings
To get access to the inner circle
To preen in front of cameras.

The cruellest season? No.
Stirring this dull protest with spring rain?
And in the streets still
do we not see the roots
That clutch out of the cages
Erected on this rubbish bluestone?

Do they know? I whisper to myself,
From this dark, hidden eyrie,
That the spell of democracy is gone.
Still I dream of Prague in '89.
A symphony of jangling keys
Announcing the accession
Of power suborned to truth.

But the speakers of the times
The gatekeepers of misinformation

The smart-suited pedlars
Of the regime narrative
They will not allow a civic forum
To meet in their metaverse.

History is not a story of development
But decay and degeneration,
Sometimes a rare birth in this fallen world.
A never-ending *Götterdamerung*.
Who am I to speak of hope?
The cycle. The wheel of fortune's malice
Stopping in this broken city.

There are those who still wear masks.
Who urge the PCR test on
every sneezing fallen being.
Who stand with Dan, and repeat the lines
At every waking meeting.
Who sneer at those who left the cage,
Anti-vaxxers, alt-right, and worse.
Who declare their membership
In the new Union of Soviet Writers.
The lockdown crusaders answered
Urban's call to build back better
To extinguish the infidels
Who do not follow the science

Who mock Saint Fauci and Brother Brett

The regime chimes poison the air,
Summon Victorians to their Hamlin duty.
To check-in, every time.
To go to a test, every time.
To substitute this message
For the signals of your own body
The workings of your own mind
The movement of your own conscience
That once inhabited your soul.
Only the government-issued test knows best.

And take the vaccine, despite your doubts.
Do not listen to any facts,
But those you hear on approved channels,
In relentless ads you paid for with your mind

The parasites of the regime
Built their careers on those ads
On their behavioural insights into your soul.

They urge you on.
Despise and hate
Those who have some doubts
Whose bodies already learned

How to calm this dragon particle-cloud.

Canto IX

Ezra speak to me now,
your persecuted thoughts,
your caged Cantos,
even the radio speeches,
those words that betrayed a nation betrayed.

The new Puritans will condemn me,
even for saying your name.
So, I will whisper it quietly here.
Ezra, you showed me again
what I have so long known.
There is always some truth in madness,
and much madness in some truths.

I sing like you from a cage.
Expecting ignominy.
Expecting my name to be cast
from the shard of the broken pot.
I do not know if these prophecies and terrors
are demons or the voices of gods.

There is no way to make the generals stop
this endless war against the virus,
its chameleon variants,

the disease of possibility.
They will besiege this city of ashes
until the earth opens beneath their clay feet.

Canto X

The tyranny drags on, but in the distance
The tyres swoosh and engines purr.
They recall an Unreal City from its exile.
Yet I know I can never return.
Not to a workplace of QR codes
and desk-booking apps.
Not to rostered days
when closeted cliques
Gather in their whispered tones.
Exiled at home, again.

I turn to my only friends:
The words, the melodies, the traces
of past dead lives who aspired to speak
in this infinite conversation
where we do not cling to esteem
nor fear rebuke;
where we give
our voice
to this never silent morning.

Red felt-tipped spikes of green stand.
Shake in the wind. Not tipped in blood,
but boldness, bravado.

The scarlet velvet of a bordello
in this suburban plain.
They stand lonely, separated,
these soul-plants.
In a dump, but striving to heaven.
In a single, narrow stalk.
They give in to no propaganda.
No talk of staying together by being apart.

This summer they redden and swell
on the spur of my moulded mount.
They guard my unvisited door.
They signal courage to the world.
They say, 'I am dangerous.'

Canto XI

Melbourne, city of grid iron streets,
Here is the place for a fake poet's ending.
Down a stale well-hole,
masked and cowered,
sinks the false poet to his ending.

*'Spiritual regeneration occurs naturally among the
poor and humble.'*

We, who stand in this broken city,
wake and dream of regeneration.

We know of no place where we can hide
from your data miners, your signal detectors,
the mistaken impossibility of your enterprise.

We are commanded by your years,
your echoes of justice.
Only the early wattle that I steal
from across the neighbour's fence
reminds me that spring will come.

We find some unbearable quiet here
where the tree roots grip the clay

in their strangling love
where the pink heath discards its bells
on this unloved soil.

Regeneration?
I look inside myself and discover nothing.
My grove will grow again
only after the fire has burned
all I have known to ash.

Principles were yesterday's guides.
Now I must find my way
through this feral city
with no compass.

I walk the streets of Melbourne
where druggies cluster everywhere.
I once knew the bustle
of suited networks in this town.
Now the shops are boarded.
Underground construction everywhere.
But it brings no beauty,
only scaffolds and mud.

This morning I am sunk in my words.
I see no way forward.

My feet scream of my worn-out bones,
ground down by long mask-free walks
to defy the tyrants' rules
on the allocated exercise hour each day.
The pain winces
the defiance of the exile,
rattles the bars of the prison
I have chosen.

I chose exile to this deserted cell.
I cannot leave now.
The walls hardened around me,
made me into this burrowing worm.
I am alone here in my exile.
No-one visits.
There are no local shopkeepers
who greet the shadow
who walks these streets every day.

I made this cell of my own free will.
Now everything darkens around me.

Was my dream of regeneration
an illusion of escape?

Will this cell bury me?

When its walls of books fall down?
To leave me only my stuttering speech,
My list of unwritten books.

Canto XII

There were the jailers, who checked in,
wore their masks, reported the young
people who dared have fun with friends.

They were assigned their role.
They took to it with passion,
just as Zimbardo wanted,
in that Stanford Prison.

And there were the prisoners,
infected failures of social distancing.
They who breathed miscreant air.
They who exposed themselves
to the all-too-human sickness.

There were fewer prisoners than jailers
in this city's prison.
But the jailers talked up the threat
if only to conceal
their residence in jail.

When it came to the vote,
most residents of the prison
believed they were jailers,

not prisoners.

They voted to keep the rules.
They voted to affirm their prison.
They voted to conceal their mistakes.
They voted for General Jaruszelski
and they voted for themselves.
Who cares what poets and freedom parties
have to say?
The donkey vote made him.
And nine per cent spoiled their ballot.

Democracy is a dangerous delusion.
The masks came back.
And calls to mask the public.

I know I am rebuffed.
I make my way, shamed,
ostracised, as an internal exile.

My beliefs are not accepted.
They cannot be known.

Society scorns me.
But in all societies
there are crevices in the ruins.

There strange new weeds grow.
There I call home.

Out of weeds we dream renewal
in these one-party states.

Canto XIII

The year of war followed
the years of plague,
and I became
more than internal exile,

more even than enemy of the state.
Released from all
obligation to obey,
I was made free.

I merely glanced at the news headlines,
knew there is no truth in the news,
and no news in the truth.
The latest manipulations
missed their mark,
if I was even the target.
I knew they did not
aim to convince me.

My thirty years
searching in the Castle
meant nothing.
I was forgotten and despised.
But now, in exile,

my mind turned to higher things.
Art and wisdom and history.
Still, I wanted more life
in the infinite conversation.
It is all fallen. There is no redemption.

Culture is the river.
Politics is the feral city
at the mouth of the river.
Religion is the mountain
from where people believe uncertainly
that the river springs.
So I said. Someone heard.

In my reordered study,
I look out at the glare in the trees.
I hear the calls of the small birds.
I know I will never be welcome
in this city again.
I know the war has made me
a traitor to my country,
at least in their eyes,
because I am a servant of wisdom.

Have I left the cage?
Or has the internment only begun?

Will my fate be scorched
on this new prison plain?

My mad but better maker,
tell me: how I can endure
the trials, the persecution,
the exile that is to come.

Is it, as you sang in that US Army base,
that what I lovest well
will not be reft from me?

Or is your troubadour lament
the grand illusion of a deluded poet?
Was your madness
the last rage to order the sense of Europe?
Should I abandon you,
like Lear in the storm?

And if I am to live
in this cage
for eleven years
like the Pandavas in the forest

Then what is *dharma*?

If I live to find another way
after the Western dream,
transported to this penisolate isle,
where *condottieri* rule,

Then what is *dharma*?

If I decouple from America,
If I spurn that empire of lies,
mongrel Reich of truant empires
on which the sun was never to set,

Then what is *dharma*?

If I believe Seymour Hersh,
and the rest who are despised
by the virtual reality state
that mobilises fools as conscript warblers,

Then what is *dharma*?

If I fall into the spying eyes
of the new progressive police state,
if I am flagged on the threat watch-list
for listening to Russians with attitude,

Then what is *dharma*?

If I am banned, cancelled and deplatformed,
demonetised and shadow-banned,
restricted, throttled, and left to languish
in my echo-chamber of hate,

Then what is *dharma*?

And if the war gets real again,
with no more phoney pretence,
no more proxies, no Potëmkin shields,
then they will declare me enemy of state,

And so what then, then what is *dharma*?

Do I turn to you, Ezra?
Or to Ugrasravas the Suta?
And what will Lord Krishna
sing as I wait for words in my chariot?

Are these broken songs my *dharma*?

Du Fu witnessed the press-ganged
seekers for glory for Ukraine
in broken, dusty wagons.

He heard the laments of mothers
who want only daughters,
even it they will be captive alienated brides.
War is fact. Peace is a desire.
The scholars wring their hands.
The soldiers know, all men must die.
War keeps its brutal science away
from the gossiping court.
I watch myself breaking in history's mirror.
Will any of these words
outlast my imprisonment
in this cage?

Other Songs

A Quiet Ordinary Life

'There was no fury in transcendent forms
But his actual candle blazed with artifice."
(Wallace Stevens, 'A quiet normal life')

The feet of the child rings the bells
Nestled in the banked paths of the city park

The sounds of Sunday walkers
Mingle like fractals of the federated square

Bikes swish over the crushed stone
In the distance, family jazz

Is mechanically reproduced.

Whistles come from nowhere
like a Borgesian list.

Traffic and trains clatter by
To make their forgotten timetable.

And the water loves the river bank
Forever beyond the band.

Children roll down the hill

They trip and trigger
The rhythms of uncertain thought

It is here, this setting, this time.
The child says, 'People are ordinary art.'

The Bird Song Outside

Late morning carols,
a gang of noisy mynahs
intimidate the peace of forest.
Magpie melodies break
the frozen silence.
In this room
the song returns.
It echoes.
The song returns
from oblivion.
The great seclusion
silenced the city.
In the days of business,
I had lost
the song of the birds.
The crows are there too.
I attend, drink in the caws,
prick up my ears
to listen. I wait
for the angelic messages.
Sounds falls into this primed bell,
this engine of meaning.
Now, from the silenced roads,
the lorikeets resume

their manic dreams,
their everlasting chatter.
Their fidget-widget whirling spin.
Iambic chirrups come
from an unknown soldier.
The birds are never only birds.
They intermingle with other souls
in my anthology of remembrance.
These singers stood on the shelf,
unsorted, neglected in possession.
A lonely crow marks out his terrain.
The blackbird flashes its perspective.
The pigeon coos in its search for seed.
The society of birds, my only cold company.
Each morning I listen
to their silly love songs.
I open one late notebook at random.
The bird itself cannot be seen.
It hides somewhere
in the green leaves
of a neighbour's tree.
The world beyond these word-lined walls
seeds the theatre of nature.
I know I can never capture these songs.
Messiaen's transcription is beyond my power.
Yet I know if I wait ,

with a still mind,
each morning,
the bush will overwhelm the city.
The forest will find my library.
The birds will save the silenced city.

Defeat is not an option

We have exiled dangerous.
Exiled naivété.
Lockdown excludes all doubts
that we control our lives.
The virus will not defeat us,
so the mantra goes.
Invincibility before death,
that old saw that fooled
every emperor become a god.

Three Forgotten Ancient Muses

Melete: Meditation.
Mneme: Remembrance.
Aoede: Song

The tenth Muse, Sappho.
Her lines of literary women:
de la Garde Deshodières
de Saurday, Queen Christina,
Hannah More.

Writing is a practice
descended from buried Muses.
The whole brood, nine and ten,
their sons and daughters,
walk the earth undead.

Melete holds the mind.
Mneme tethers the mind to time.
Aoede releases the mind in breath.

Fecund daughters of Memory.

The solidarity of the shattered

When you have not slept,
when darkness fills you
all the way down,
when before the day begins
you throw your last.

When the black clouds
steeple inside, then dump
a never ending storm,
when Everyman speaks Babel
and Everywoman sings pain.

Then stand alone and defiant,
silenced and still speaking,
even if others fell to their knees,
succumbed to masks and jeering
by Jaruselszki in his North Face blue.

Stand and wait for ice to fill you.
Become a frozen shard,
sharpened danger
To they who would destroy
The solidarity of the shattered

Orpheus in Melbourne

I remember the years when I left
this garden. Before its vines,
its flowers, its stone, its rotting mulch
enclosed me in infernal safety.

There was a city of glass shards,
bluestone walls and cafe laneways
where I would walk in a suit
and breathe the same air,

touch the same bitumen,
hold common door handles,
brush the same vitreous glass,
perch on dying leather stools,
served with the same bitter drinks,

dwell in the same house of being
as these icons I share on screen
yet who I do not know
except as wraiths

from the other world
I still remember.

I remember still when I allowed
the angel face to guide me here.
I barely knew then, as I descended,
that I may not return to the former world,

where life contended with life,
And did not freeze death in a plastic mould.
The angel, who was soon joined
by a swarm of lesser cherubs

who bore their darts of love,
who chanted favoured words in chorus,
told me: Do not look back.
You will not return to the upper world.

Infected with simple life and virtue,
we will build a better world,
here behind our screens,
masked by our burning truths.

Do not look back.
Do not return.

I remember now the accidents of life.
The risks I took crossing the road,
walking into a shop,

unscanned and unmasked,
mingling with the unclean,
the distrusted and untested citizens
of this Unreal City.

I could not know
fear of death would undo so many.

Here in the lower circle
there are no risks.
Or so the angels say.
There are no unplanned meetings.

No long lost friends encountered
when leaving lunch at that new place.
Just the same routine, every day.
The only adventure is how
to evade the rules in vicarious protest.

I remember now there is a burning library,
deep within this garden.
And there I can encircle my sufferings
in magic flames to seal off
the jabbering chorus of angels.

In the flames, I lie in state,

await my ascent, without regret,
to the upper world
where I will sing again
of the ruined city of ashes,
the fellowship of cold skulls
that I discovered here,
among my weeds and discarded habits,
carried by a black cockatoo
to the hall of the skalds.

The Way to Kunlun

Why do the soft rain and the free bird song
show me the way in the unfallen world?
Speak to me of riding the wind this morning?

This year Kunlun is my home,
my shield, my station,
where I will walk alone,
stripped of the lies of power,
unmasked to show my face
to my rare companion
who speaks from beneath
the soil of infinite conversation.

Holy Mother (Russia)

They try to tear my foster mother apart
from the lands in which she bled and prayed,
planted the wheat, mined the salt,
lay down in frozen tears,
mingled with the black earth.

They mistake those lands for a chessboard.
They misconstrue nightmares as strategy.
They imagine they are the grand masters.
But do not know the strength
and reach of the Mother.

My own mother lost her mind
before she lost her life.
The Holy Mother sustained me in madness,
in grief, amidst the ashes,
of the outcast prophet,
cancelled from this time and all time,
or so they try.
But preserved by the Angels of Peter.

Now she is besieged, again,
by a pirate empire that dare not say its name.
That sails with a lying flag.

Where sky is black, and wheat is blood.
And the dark sun shows its shame again.

The looters will discover
the Holy Mother has secured her cache.
She has planted her feet bravely
in the steppe and in the taiga,
in the ice and in the salt,
in the White and the Black Seas.
There she stands with her hands of мир
Encircling the world island.

I long from afar,
on this southern barren island,
impotent outcast that I am,
to stand in the fire of Kali's womb,
to dance to death
the plastic fake Western tomb.

Cat Nap

The cat sinks into my lap.
He demands this luxury every morning.
His chin rests on my patella.
His eyes squeeze into acceptance.
What is on his cat-mind?

My mind is more febrile than feline.
It whirs while my companion purrs.
My endless questions do not disturb
the peace of my cat's laptop nap.

I get up to make coffee.
Try to place my cat in the deep armchair.
He springs from the luxury,
and makes his way to the door,

Where, beyond the exit in sunshine,
He asks me, 'Have you washed your bowl?'

Observing the Storm

First the phone alert from the weather man
warned me of severe thunderstorms.

Then I could see the mourning clouds
approach my library tower from the East.

I was learning new Russian words,
when the storm drained all light from the sky.

I looked up thunder and lightning
in my русский словарь, and tried to go on.

Shvarts' strange religion danced in my room,
but darkness dragged me into the storm.

I put my book down and just stopped.
Cold air streamed in, over my кошка's purr.

I slowed down. I just watched the storm
roll over my home. The rain came down.

The thunder rumbled through.
Dull lightning flashed.
I could do nothing but watch

as the storm subsided.

The ambulance sirens
returned me to this day.

This is how tragedy happens,
beyond the vision of the grand masters.

How to Make a Life

I

Not in circumstances of your own
making as if the real
was free of madness.

You never know
whether to break the rules
or obey tradition

the long river that tethers
past to present
blessing to catastrophe

where sails trade and war
disease and invasion
faith and the curse of ideas.

II

With passion and purpose
as if our fate
lay in our hands

our daemons were discovered

speaking truth to power
perched on our shoulders

like an imprisoned angel
who lost the power of flight
and decided to stick it out

come what may, through thick and thin,
seeing through this choice
they did not make. But must endure.

III

By stooping to drink from the slow river
as if anyone has time
for that today.

When humility has become another brand
and there are no quiet spots
left on earth

where the psyche can build its tower
from stone shaped by hand
in a lonely perfect circle.

Still, the clear water flows on,

while we chatter on the banks,
onto the harbour we fear to know.

IV

Through some kind of *amor mundi*
as if the world
deserved our love.

Not our critique and contempt
and constant claims for change
our clamour for the conquest

by the last ideas
of this frail imagined world
that will survive beyond our fall

in the flow of an inherited dream
whose meaning we never know
even, at the end, as we sink into its depths.

Dr Cogito Plots Revenge

Dr Cogito serves his scraps
onto the old tin plates

in battered hands
of surly men

behind the masked face
he dreams

of recipes
of the magnificent casserole.

Garden Tanka

1. Fallen Leaves

Flower collectors
Stand on the soft fallen leaves
Clothing the stony path
That marks the last boundary
Of your neglected garden.

2. Gentle Birds

From unknown perches
Crows and some gentler birds
Sing lost melodies
While I travel with Heaney
To the Ministry of Fear.

3. Last Ride

I lift my daughter
For the last time to the train;
She rides to the city
Where her career in law begins
While my ostracism endures.

4. Winter Chill

The ghost gum quivers
In the sudden winter chill
As I look down on
Two lines of newly planted
Silver and beloved hermits.

5. Yellow Spears

Bird song breaks the cold night
Forgotten now in glaring brick
And my glance at yellow spears
Is soon pierced by sirens faraway.

6. Faraway Sirens

The glaring brick blinds
Bird song breaks the colder night
My glance, at these spears
Of yellow, defeated fear,
Pierced by sirens faraway.

7. Broken Buds

Wattle birds dive through
The Autumn's golden bubbles
The Fall of Kabul
Echoes in my broken buds
Then a white cockatoo shrieks.

8. White Wood

White wood with peach peel
Faded, torn in this modest trunk
Rises from blue bells
Reflects the studio sun
Stands guard for contemplation

9. Ten Children

The ten children who died
In America's war crime
To strike for wounded
Pride, for a broken empire:
Now we know, we must go elsewhere.

10. Red Spike

The red spike rises
Where the wattle bird sings
Yearning for sun. Gloom and mind
Swell like thunderstorms.
In the coven the shadow bird hides alone.

11. Black Cockatoo

When the machines stop
The birds' singing begins, I hear
Their warbling and trills
But the black cockatoo's screech
Soars across this blue-sky day.

12. Overhead Wires

Two magpies perch on
The overhead wires. Their song
Pierces the grey sky.
In my ears, the wars drone on
In my hands are only words.

13. Hand Writing

There will come a day
When Youtube falls and Twitter
Dies, and on that day
This handwritten poem will
Be here, ever flowering.

14. Dead Heroes

I put black plugs in my ear.
Stories of war flood in.
I take the plugs out.
Black cockatoos fly across
The sky, dead heroes in claw.

15. Dread Spreads

It returned last night
Every it there can be.
Black dread spread all over me.
My eyes did not close because
It prowled into my body.

16. Wattle Bird

The wattle bird feeds
Among the white gum's thin leaves
Then springs away to
Another garden tended
By solitary viewers.

17. Golden Wattle

The Golden Wattle
Beneath old leucoxylon
I planted for him.
Distant mufflers drone below
The magpie's morning carol.

18. Summer Heat

The first summer heat bakes
White wood eucalypt, planted
Years before, beneath
This room where I write
Forgiven forms, cat on lap.

19. Nature Remade

In street, repairs end.
Talk begins. Mowers silence
Brief revelation.
We remade nature. Cities
Now rule. We lie in our beds.

20. Mynah Birds

The mynah birds screech
Then carillon bells
Bounce between tree tops
Before the jackdaw crows
To announce the coming storm.

21. Mynah Birds

The mowers start up.
Then one hot day in December
Brings blue sun-scorched winds.
My eyes weep with hay fever, and
Memory of war.

Afterword: Five Years After Lockdown

I have published these poems with all their imperfections later than I had first intended. They were written mostly between 2020 and 2022. I prepared them for publication in mid-2023. But then I hesitated.

I knew the poems could be refined as literature. But literary reputation was not the reason I published these cries from a cage. I could polish these texts with literary sheen. But pursuit of the esteem of academic critics was not the reason I paused.

I wanted to publish these poems with all their faults because, as Illidan Stormrage says at the climax of a popular computer game story, "I am my scars." The scars in these poems were also not only mine, but were shared by millions, if not billions, of people around the world. We all experienced the trauma of lockdown together. We all knew that our screams of pain had been suppressed. I could not accept that those screams and the quieter poems of recovery would be suppressed forever.

But in mid-2023 those scars were still, open, raw and salted by orthodox opinion. Public inquiries into what went wrong during the COVID years largely whitewashed the political, public health and community responses. Conversations about the matter were difficult. Voluntary censorship still prevailed.

New demands emerged that the community speak with one voice. The conflict in Ukraine continued. The genocide in Gaza ground on. In both cases, darks clouds of thought control hovered dissidents. People were smeared, defamed, deplatformed and even, in some cases, killed. These poems were an intentional act of rebellion, in crafted uncontrolled phrasing, against that thought control. Publishing these poems would be a further act of defiance. But would it provoke pain? Would it bring me and my loved ones into danger. I hesitated.

I began to wonder whether I did not just want to let go of the pain. After all, there are things a healthy mind just forgets. After every war, Szymborska writes, someone must clean up; to pick up all the rants and raves, scribbled on paper, and throw it all into the bin. Memory can bring relentless pain. History can reactivate grievance. Sometimes forgetting is the best act of forgiveness.

Consumed by these chilling fears, my plan, to publish and be damned, froze. The book sat on my computer in a state of ninety per cent completion. Meanwhile, life moved on. My writing turned away from lyric poems towards poetic essays and commentary on war descending into a new kind of global war and diplomacy degenerating into narcissistic aggression. The pain of those years of lockdown faded. The outrage at what happened dissipated. The habit of writing poetry left me as I vested my prose commentary with poetic charges. Was I even a poet anymore? What was the point of publishing those poems?

I had wondered, since the lockdown era ended in early 2022, when the great art of the period would emerge. In the early months of 2025, I began to see fiction, television dramas and other works that began to dramatize life in this era in ways that broke from the imprisoned emotions of the cage. The war fever that had washed over the West began to fade. The opposition to the horrors of Gaza grew. The thought control complex began to crack.

Through one of those fissures, I received a comment from a reader as the Australian summer came to a close, five years after the start of the lockdown years. The reader asked me to publish the poems to honour the experience of the suffering imprisoned and the stifled voices. The simple, honest request broke the last lock that had caged these cantos.

I pushed open the gate of the cage. I finished this story and, without looking back over the poems, despite all their flaws, shared these cantos with a world at war.

About the Author

Jeff Rich is a poet, author, historian, and content creator. He lives in Melbourne, Australia. His writing, commentary, and videos are gathered at www.jeffrich.substack.com and @theburning archive

His previous collection of poetry was *Gathering Flowers of the Mind: Collected Poems, 1996-2020* (2021).

His prose collections are *From the Burning Archive: Essays and Fragments, 2015-2022* (2022) and *Thirteen Ways of Looking at a Bureaucrat: Writing on Governing* (2023).